Why
Do People Abuse
Human Rights?

Ali Brownlie

 Raintree

Chicago, Illinois

© 2005 Raintree
Published by Raintree
a division of Reed Elsevier, Inc.
Chicago, Illinois
Customer Service 888-363-4266
Visit our website at www.raintreelibrary.com

Every effort has been made to trace copyright holders of any material reproduced in this book. Any omissions will be rectified in subsequent printings if notice is given.

Library of Congress Cataloging-in-Publication Data:
Brownlie, Alison, 1949-
    Why do people abuse human rights? / Ali Brownlie.
        v. cm. -- (Exploring tough issues)
    Includes bibliographical references and index.
    Contents: Understanding human rights -- The right to life -- Why are children's
  rights abused -- Why are workers' rights abused -- Why are human rights
  abused in time of conflict -- Less than human? -- Claiming and upholding human
  rights.
    ISBN 0-7398-6684-2 (Library binding-hardcover)
    1. Human rights--Juvenile literature.   [1. Human rights.]   I. Title. II. Series.
  JC571.B72 2004
  323--dc22

2003020108

08 07 06 05 04
10 9 8 7 6 5 4 3 2 1

Printed by C&C Offset Printing Co., Ltd, China

Picture acknowledgments
The publisher would like to thank the following for their kind permission to use their pictures: p. 4 Hodder Wayland Picture Library (Gordon Clements); pp. 5, 16, 25, 29, 38, 39, 40 Exile Images (Howard Davies); p. 6 Popperfoto/Reuters (Ulli Michel); p. 7 Rex Features (Don Cravens, Timepix); p. 8 Exile Images (J. Etchart); pp. 9, 10 Rex Features (Sipa); p. 11 Popperfoto/Reuters (Danilo Krstanovic); p. 12 Popperfoto/Reuters (A. Weerawong); p. 13 Popperfoto/Reuters (Dan Chung); pp. 14, 19 Popperfoto/Reuters (Jim Bourg); p. 15 Rex Features (Timepix); p. 17 Hodder Wayland Picture Library (Howard Davies); p. 18 Hodder Wayland Picture Library (Angela Hampton); p. 20 Rex Features (Denis Cameron); pp. 21, 23 Popperfoto/Reuters (Brad Bower); pp. 22, 31 Topham/ImageWorks; p. 24 Popperfoto/Reuters (David Gray); p. 26 Popperfoto/Reuters (Guy Wathen); p. 27 Popperfoto/Reuters (Kim Kyung-hoon); pp. 28, 30 Popperfoto/Reuters (Vasily Fedosenko); p. 32 Popperfoto/Reuters (Jim Hollander); p. 33 Popperfoto/Reuters (US DoD); p. 34 Mary Evans Picture Library; pp. 35, 41 Rex Features; p. 36 Popperfoto/Reuters (Erik de Castro); p. 37 Popperfoto/Reuters (Sayed Salahuddin); p. 42 Popperfoto/Reuters (Ian Waldie); p. 43 Hodder Wayland Picture Library; p. 44 Popperfoto/Reuters (Nick Sharp); p. 45 Exile Images (C. Smith).

Cover picture: Workers, including a young girl, carry bundles of wood off a boat on the Tonle Sap River in Cambodia. (Corbis).

Contents

1. Understanding Human Rights

All people have human rights simply because they are human beings. It makes no difference who they are, where they live, or what they do. Human rights are like a set of rules that apply to everyone. Frequently, however, the rules are broken and human rights are violated and abused. Sometimes this is done by individuals or groups of people, but sometimes it is done by governments.

There is no single reason why people treat other human beings badly. On some occasions people do it on purpose because they are greedy and want to gain power or money. Some people actually like causing unhappiness to others. Feelings of fear, violence, and cruelty are part of all human beings in varying degrees.

◀ These Maasai people are collecting water from a well. The right to clean water is denied to many people in the world as a result of both poverty and conflict.

Sometimes people infringe upon others' human rights through ignorance; they do not understand what the consequences of their actions will be. Sometimes human rights are violated when one person's rights are given priority over another person's rights.

People often talk about the rights they think they have. They say they have a "right" to smoke or to own a gun. These are not really "rights" but things that people may be allowed to do by local or national laws. In these cases they have a legal right, but this is not the same as a universal human right. In other countries, in fact, such activities may be against the law. It is important to understand the difference between those things that all human beings need, which should be rights, and what some people would like to have or to do.

Many people have fought and struggled for their own rights and the rights of others, sometimes at great cost to themselves.

"We hold these truths to be self-evident; that all men are created equal, that they are endowed by their creator with certain unalienable rights, that among these are life, liberty, and the pursuit of happiness."
U.S. Declaration of Independence

◀ *Aung San Suu Kyi addresses a rally outside her home in Rangoon, Myanmar (Burma). She has led the peaceful resistance to the military regime in Myanmar, denouncing it as a government that has abused human rights.*

5

How did human rights come about?

Human rights are not something new. Thousands of years ago in the ancient civilizations of Babylon, China, and India, people talked about human rights. Human rights have always been central to the teachings of the world's major religions.

Before World War II (1939–1945), it was generally felt that human rights were a matter for nations to sort out for themselves. What human rights declarations there were did not include all members of society. For example, women and minority groups were often omitted. However, the atrocities and violations of human rights that took place during World War II changed worldwide opinion and made human rights a universal concern.

The people who founded the United Nations (UN) in 1945 dreamed of peace and justice through international cooperation. With this in mind the UN adopted the Universal Declaration of Human Rights (UDHR) on December 10, 1948. It is now recognized as the world's most important human rights document, and nearly every country in the world has signed it.

▲ *Nelson Mandela on his release after 27 years in prison. He stood up against the racist apartheid government of South Africa and was charged with sabotage. He became South Africa's first black president, and won the Nobel Peace prize in 1993.*

case study · case study · case study · case study · case study

In Montgomery, Alabama, during the 1960s African Americans and white Americans did not have equal rights. One way in which African Americans were discriminated against was by being forced to sit in the back of public buses as a sign of respect to white people. One hot day Rosa Parks, an African-American woman, sat at the front of the bus. The driver told her to move but she refused and so the driver called for the police. Word spread about what she had done and black people stopped using the buses. The bus companies lost a lot of money because passengers had stopped using their service. Eventually the rule was changed. This action was one of the springboards for the creation of the civil rights movement in the United States.

▶ *Rosa Parks (right) after the U.S. Supreme Court ruling that said passengers on buses should not be segregated.*

Most nations have also ratified other human rights conventions, in particular the Convention on the Rights of the Child. Unfortunately these declarations have not yet brought about an end to abuses of human rights. Since 1948 millions of people have been killed and jailed because of their origins, ideas, or beliefs and because of their struggles for justice and freedom. Every day of the year, every single one of the 30 articles in the UDHR is violated somewhere in the world.

Why abuse human rights?

It may be difficult for us to understand why anyone would abuse human rights. Some people deliberately abuse human rights because they are greedy and want power over others, or because by abusing others they can make gains for themselves. Some people abuse an individual or a group's rights because they don't believe the person or group deserves to have basic rights. An abuser may believe he or she deserves to have power over someone who is older, younger, weaker, or just plain different from him or herself. Many people have an unfounded fear or dislike of those who are different from themselves.

There are also occasions where people feel forced to abuse someone else's human rights. This may be because they are trying to protect themselves and their family. Sometimes a human right is abused because the abuser believes that what he or she is doing is morally right and in the interests of the greater good. For example, a police officer may violate an individual's right to privacy in an attempt to catch a criminal.

▲ *People in Chile protest against General Pinochet, a man who has been accused of many human rights abuses. The sign reads, "No to the devil."*

Sometimes people try to excuse human rights violations by saying that they are for the common good. In 2002 the Israeli army entered Palestinian villages and towns, bulldozed houses, and shot and arrested young men. The Israelis justified this action by arguing that it was necessary to prevent further suicide bomb attacks on Israeli civilians. This puts the rights of one group of people above those of another. Some people would argue that no abuse of human rights can be justified.

▲ *An Israeli soldier stands by while a digger removes the rubble of the demolished headquarters of the Palestinian Authority in the West Bank town of Hebron.*

2.The Right to Live

Is it always wrong to abuse the right to live?

Article 3 of the UDHR states that we all have the right to life, liberty, and security of person. Many people believe that life is the most important right anyone can have and that it is never right to take another life.

Usually the taking of a human life is a criminal offense and is considered morally wrong, but there are exceptions. It is not always against the law and killing is sometimes justified on moral grounds. War and capital punishment are examples where killing is allowed by governments. However, today capital punishment is practiced in only a few countries. In some cases self-defense is recognized by the law as a justifiable excuse for killing another person, although it is often hard to prove.

◀ *The aftermath of a suicide bombing on a bus in Haifa, Israel, in 2002. Terrorists who commit such acts believe that the taking of human life is justified if it helps the cause that they are fighting for.*

A Bosnian woman cries over her son's coffin. Her son was a soldier killed by Serbs near Mostar in 1996.

In the past, in some small nomadic groups of people, geriatricide (killing of the old) was practiced. When times were hard and food was in short supply, elderly people were left behind when the group moved on. They would be given a small supply of food but had little hope of surviving. This was not viewed as a sign of disrespect for the elderly, and they understood that it ensured the survival of the rest of the group.

How can we distinguish between murder, manslaughter, capital punishment, killing in self-defense, and killing during times of war when we are trying to decide whether the right to live has been abused? Some people argue that taking someone's life is always a violation of their right to live whatever the circumstances. But is it always wrong to kill?

> FACT:
> As many as 15 million children die every year from preventable diseases—2.2 million alone from the effects of diarrhea.
> *Save The Children*

The right to live vs. the quality of life

While many people think that the right to live is something that should never be violated, others argue that the quality of life is just as important, if not more so. Think of someone who has a terminal illness and is suffering in great pain. Should they have the right to die?

A subject that arouses great controversy is euthanasia—helping people who want to die to do so. If someone has given his or her permission, is it still wrong to assist the person in dying? People with certain religious beliefs would say it is, while others may say it is the right or moral thing to do. Friends and relatives of elderly people have sometimes helped them to die, or have even killed them in what they argue is an act of mercy.

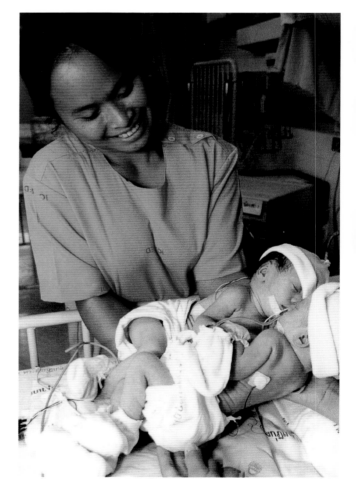

▶ *Conjoined twins at a Bangkok hospital in 1998. Sometimes one twin has to be sacrificed in order for the other one to live.*

case study · case study · case study · case study · case study

In 2001 a British woman, Diane Pretty, went to the European Court of Human Rights to argue the case that her husband should be able to help her die without being prosecuted for doing so. She was terminally ill with motor neuron disease and had decided she did not want to live any longer and eventually die in pain. She lost her case. The ruling was that she did not have the right to die through the active intervention of another person.

▶ *Diane Pretty and her husband Brian after the verdict of the European Court of Human Rights.*

A 76-year-old man in Florida shot his wife who had a terminal illness. He did it, he claimed, because he loved her and could not bear to see her suffering. He was sentenced to 25 years in prison without parole, although he was released five years later.

The issue centers on the degree to which life must be protected and the need to allow people to die with dignity and without suffering. Is euthanasia an act of kindness and compassion, or an act of murder and a violation of human rights?

The state and the right to life

China is one of the countries that still uses the death penalty. This women was convicted of murder and is being taken to be executed.

During 2001 over 3,000 people were killed legally by their governments through the use of the death penalty. This is practiced in more than 30 countries for crimes that range from murder and treason to adultery. The countries that inflict capital punishment most are China, Iran, Saudi Arabia, and the United States.

Supporters of capital punishment argue that the state should have the right to take measures that break the terms of the Universal Declaration of Human Rights. They argue that the death penalty discourages those who may murder in the future. It is also justified in terms of being "an eye for an eye," meaning that if one life is taken, it is acceptable to take another as punishment. Some argue that murderers, who take away an individual's right to life, don't deserve to have their own rights recognized.

However, those who are against such punishment point out that there is no evidence to show that the death penalty has reduced the murder rate. The United States, which has the death penalty, has a murder rate that is three times that of Great Britain, where there is no death penalty. Those opposed to the death penalty also express concern that people are given the death penalty unfairly. More African Americans are sentenced to death than white people who commit the same crime. There is also a concern that innocent people are executed. According to the American Civil Liberties Union, more than 100 innocent people have been released from death row since 1978.

> "Our present system of capital punishment violates our basic belief in justice and equality and places us among the world's worst abusers of human rights."
>
> *Jesse Jackson Jr., U.S. Congressman*

▼ *A prisoner sits in his cell on death row in Angola State Prison, Louisiana.*

FACT:
In 2001, 66 prisoners were executed in the United States, bringing the total to 785 since 1976.
Amnesty International

3. Why Are Children's Rights Abused?

Children's rights—special rights?

Children, as human beings, are entitled to basic human rights, although in the best interests of the child, adults usually make decisions on their behalf. What happens to a child in her or his early years will influence the rest of his or her life. Children need good nutrition, education, and care. According to the United Nations, about 150 million children in the world under the age of five are malnourished. This is a direct result of poverty, one of the most common obstacles to the enjoyment of basic human rights.

Like other groups in society that lack power and are vulnerable, children are often denied their rights. They have little say in things that affect them. They are often expected to do things and are treated in a way that would be seen as an abuse of rights if an adult were treated in the same way. Examples range from not being listened to or taken seriously to being forced to work in terrible conditions or to fight in wars.

▲ *Children need special care. This child is being weighed as part of a program in Kenya run by Médecins sans Frontières (Doctors without Borders), an international medical aid organization.*

Children are denied some of the rights adults have because they are thought to be too young to be able to exercise them responsibly without special protection. For instance, children are not allowed to vote or get married under a certain age. This age varies from country to country.

> "The principle of 'all children, all rights' is still too far from being a reality."
>
> *Kofi Annan, UN Secretary General*

Clearly, children need special protection. For this reason, in 1989, the United Nations adopted the Convention on the Rights of the Child. It recognized the important differences between adults and children. All but two of the world's 193 nation states, the United States and Somalia, have ratified and signed the Convention. The U.S. government believes that the Convention undermines parental rights.

▼ *These children are playing soccer. The Convention on the Rights of the Child says that all children should have the right to play.*

Child cruelty and abuse

Children are dependent on the adults who look after them. This dependency, and their lack of physical power, make children particularly vulnerable to physical and sexual abuse and neglect. Sometimes children are beaten, forced into sexual acts, or not provided with proper food, warmth, shelter, clothing, care, and love.

While the vast majority of adults who look after children do a good job, there are a few who abuse the trust that children and society place in them. Shockingly it is sometimes the parents who are responsible for child abuse. Foster parents, clergy, teachers, and neighbors are also among the adults who have been convicted of abusing children.

There is evidence to show that some abused children go on to be abusive parents, and that some sex offenders, particularly those who target children, experienced sexual and physical abuse in their own childhood. However, other children suffer terrible childhoods but do not grow up to be abusers themselves.

▶ *This child has Down's Syndrome. Children with disabilities may be targeted by bullies in school, or less able to defend themselves against abusive adults.*

In many countries where it would be illegal to hit an adult, it is permissible to hit children as a form of punishment. How and when adults can do this to children depends on the national laws.

▲ Protesters demonstrate against the sexual abuse of children by members of the clergy in Boston.

Children themselves sometimes abuse the rights of other children, particularly through bullying and name-calling. Bullies may sometimes be people with a low opinion of themselves. Bullying can be a way to try to hide this from other people. As with adults, though, some child bullies are those who believe they have special, or more, rights than their peers.

FACT:
On any one day in the United States it is estimated that over 3,000 school students will experience some form of physical punishment.

Child labor

During the 1800s in England and the United States some children were made to work in factories, mines, and mills for up to twelve hours a day. Because they were small, they were made to crawl into cramped places to do difficult and dangerous work. Many children were injured or killed. Children were cheap to employ and the factory owners made good money.

Today about 250 million children between five and seventeen years old work worldwide, often in conditions no better, and sometimes worse, than those experienced by children in the 1800s. Their families live in poverty and they send their children out to work at a young age. They do many different jobs. For example, they may weave carpets, where their small hands are able to do delicate work, or stitch soccer balls. They earn just a few pennies a day. Rarely are there any regulations covering the conditions in which they work. They may work for sixteen hours a day without a break.

▼ *This child works in Egypt. Even very young children may be required to operate dangerous machinery in cramped, unhealthy conditions.*

These young people are participating in the six-month Global March arriving outside the International Labour Organization headquarters in Geneva, Switzerland. Young people from all over the world joined in the march against child labor.

Grinding poverty forces these children into work, for them it is a necessity. Although child labor is against the law in countries like India, it still goes on anywhere factory owners are determined to use cheap child labor to increase their profits. People in the western world are not always aware of the role they are playing in supporting this practice when they buy products like soccer balls and sneakers. Poverty lies at the core of this abuse of human rights.

"I have been stitching soccer balls as long as I can remember. My hands are constantly in pain. It feels like they are burning."

Geeta, age eleven, India

4.Why Are Workers' Rights Abused?

Work as a right

Work is the way in which people are able to earn money to meet their basic needs and keep themselves alive. Work can also be fulfilling and contribute to a person's feelings of worth. Article 23 of the UDHR states that people should have the right to work, to do so in decent conditions, to enjoy equal pay with someone who is doing the same job, and to receive a wage that is fair for the type of work being done. The Article also states that everyone has the right to form and join a labor union. These are "economic rights."

▼ *People on their way to work in New York City. The UDHR states that everyone has a right to work.*

Protesters campaign against Coca-Cola, a company that had been accused of racial discrimination.

In most countries of the world, it is the job of the government to ensure that there is work. If the economy begins to fail, job losses follow and unemployment rises. But sometimes people find it difficult to get work even when there are plenty of jobs around. This is when it becomes a human rights issue, because it means that people are being discriminated against. This usually happens on the grounds of the race, sex, age, religion, disability, or the sexual orientation of the person seeking work.

Although in many countries it is against the law to discriminate in this way, some companies find ways around it. For example, a company in northern England did not want to hire black people, so it invented a policy of not employing people from a particular area of a city because it knew that many black people lived there. In Brazil some companies require women to produce a certificate of sterilization when applying for a job, so they will not need to have time off work to have a baby.

FACT:
In the United Kingdom black people are twice as likely to be unemployed as white people, even if they are better qualified to do a certain job.
International Labour Organization

Rights versus profit

The basic purpose of business in a capitalist system is to make a profit. Most companies recognize that to do this they must respect human rights; after all, it benefits their business in the long term to do so. But in some cases, the bosses are so driven to increase their profits and keep their own highly paid jobs that they ignore the rights of the workers.

FACT:
The largest companies in the world—such as Wal-Mart, ExxonMobil, General Motors—have revenues larger than the economies of entire middle-income countries, such as Norway, Poland, and Denmark.

At least 1.1 million people around the world die of work-related accidents and diseases each year. Even more are injured. Many of these deaths and injuries could have been prevented if the companies had spent more money and taken more care to ensure that there were adequate health and safety provisions.

◀ A May Day anti-globalization protester outside the Australian Stock Exchange in Sydney, 2001.

A protester in London demonstrates her objections to an Arms Trade Fair supported by the British government. The purpose of such fairs is to sell weapons and armaments to other countries.

The activities of one particular business may not violate human rights, but in seeking to make a bigger profit it may choose to buy its supplies from companies that do abuse rights. For instance, a company making chocolate may buy its ingredients from another company that uses forced child labor in the cocoa plantations of West Africa. Other businesses may produce products that are used to violate human rights. This is especially true of the arms industry, which produces landmines that remain lethal long after they have been laid. In the chemical and pharmaceutical industries, drugs may be tested on people in poorer countries where there are fewer regulations to protect their safety.

Labor unions

The terrible and dangerous conditions in which many people worked in the factories and workshops of 19th-century Europe led to the founding of labor unions. Workers realized that there was strength in numbers and got together to negotiate with employers for improvements in pay and conditions. They also began to put pressure on governments to create laws that would protect their rights as workers.

▶ *A miner is rescued from a flooded shaft at the Quecreek Mine in Somerset, Pennsylvania in 2002. Miners face particular dangers in their jobs.*

case study · case study · case study · case study · case study

In 1888 Anne Besant wrote a newspaper article called "White Slavery in London" about the terrible pay and dangerous conditions suffered by young women working at the Bryant and May match factory. Three girls suspected of giving her information were fired, and 1,500 women walked out in sympathy. The three girls were rehired. Many countries now have a legal minimum wage, a small formal recognition of union demands for human dignity. Today people like the girls working in the match factory who tell outsiders about abuses or wrongdoing in their workplace are known as "whistle-blowers."

Article 23 of the UDHR states that "everyone has the right to form and join a labor union...." However, forming unions has not always been easy. Although unions are there to defend the rights of workers, in some countries actually working for or belonging to a union can lead to imprisonment, torture, or even death. Even when labor unions are accepted, people can still lose their jobs or be victimized for trying to set up a union. In Colombia the leader of a paramilitary group said that labor union members should be killed because they interfered with the "orderly conduct of business."

In 1984 the British government announced that staff at GCHQ, a spy station that listens in to communications around the globe, had to resign from their union or face dismissal. The reason given by the government was that being a member of the union might be in conflict with national security. Many workers refused to give up their right to belong to a union and lost their jobs. In this instance people's right to belong to a union was considered to be less important than national security.

▶ *Members of the Federation of Korean Unions hold banners during a rally in Seoul on May 1, 2002. The demonstrators were demanding a shorter working week.*

5. Why Are Human Rights Abused in Times of Conflict?

The causes of war

War is the greatest threat to people's rights. Inevitably people are killed and injured, but there are many other human rights casualties, too. People are traumatized, and forced to leave their homes and become refugees. Freedoms are limited and severe restrictions are often put on the media to control what they are allowed to report. All wars create poverty and human suffering. In Sudan, for example, 6 million people were displaced during a conflict in the 1980s, the majority as a result of food shortages due to disruption to farming and trade.

> **FACT:**
> More than 120,000 children under the age of 18 are being used as soldiers in Africa.
> *Human Rights Watch, 1999*

◀ *During the border tension in Kashmir, a territory between India and Pakistan that both countries claim, Pakistani soldiers listen to a briefing from General Khan, 2002.*

The causes of war are complex and varied. They include conflict over land ownership, as in the dispute between India and Pakistan over Kashmir, or a battle of beliefs and ideologies, like the Korean War between the communist-backed North Korea and the United States-backed South Korea in the early 1950s. Today Korea is still divided into North and South.

Most wars have both historical and human causes. They are the result of things that have happened in the past and of how people view the current situation. On several occasions wars have been started by a single event. Old rivalries and tensions between the Hutus and Tutsis in Rwanda flared into conflict, genocide, and massacres when the president, Juvenal Habyarimana, was killed in a plane crash. Hutus suspected that this was the work of Tutsi rebels. It is estimated that more than 500,000 Rwandans died, and over half the surviving population were forced to move from their homes as a result.

"We must remember that these faithful followers [of the Fascist leaders]… were not born torturers, were not (with a few exceptions) monsters, they were ordinary men."
Italian novelist Primo Levi, survivor of Auschwitz, 1987

◀ *Rwandan refugees cross the river to Tanzania in 1994, fleeing the genocide in Rwanda where Hutus and Tutsis were killing one another.*

The human rights of civilians

Since the 20th century, civilians have increasingly become the victims of war and armed conflicts. As hand-to-hand fighting has become less common and the military makes use of long-distance rockets and bombing from the air, civilians are more often in the firing line.

Civilians are often forced to flee wars and conflict zones, becoming refugees and asylum seekers. They leave behind their homes and possessions, sometimes even their families, and become one of the world's most vulnerable groups. Many of their human rights are denied them, particularly their right to security (Article 3) and their right not to be exiled (Article 9).

Human rights are further infringed upon when a state of emergency is declared in a country. During this time the media may not be able to report what is going on, and people may be subjected to a curfew, restricting their right to freedom of movement and being part of a community.

▶ *Afghan refugees wait for food at a camp in Koja Bahuddin in northern Afghanistan in 2001. They were forced from their homes by fighting.*

FACT:
The countries that received the most refugees in 2000, relative to their total population, were Armenia, Guinea, Yugoslavia, and Congo.

"You cannot explain what it is like to be forced from your home. I just wanted to cry and never stop."

Saranda, Kosovo

The public often supports censorship in certain circumstances believing it to be in the interest of their own security. But this can be open to abuse. Organizations like Article 19, named after the relevant article in UDHR, campaign against any kind of censorship. They argue that the free reporting and investigation of issues by journalists is the cornerstone of democracy.

Journalists themselves run risks in reporting. In 1998, 50 journalists were killed around the world, 22 of them in Latin America. They were usually killed because their investigations took them too close to people who had something to lose by being exposed.

▶ A Palestinian helps a photographer who has been shot in the hand during clashes with Israeli troops in 2000.

War atrocities

Soldiers and people who serve in the military are vulnerable to human rights abuses on two fronts. On the one hand, they are put into dangerous positions where they may be ordered to commit atrocities, and on the other they are vulnerable to having their own rights abused.

When war is declared, one of the first things that may happen is that able-bodied civilians are conscripted, or drafted, into the military. Some countries accept that people have the right to refuse to fight and these people may be required to work in civilian service, such as in a hospital.

> "As a pacifist I object to any army. I will never carry a weapon and I refuse to wear a uniform or any symbol that represents or labels me as part of the army."
>
> *Yair Halper, age eighteen, imprisoned in Israel for resisting the draft*

▼ *A group of Israeli conscripts. Young people in Israel are required to serve in the military.*

In the early 1960s, a study was conducted at Yale University. Researchers found that volunteers of all ages and occupations would willingly follow orders to inflict pain on other people. Although the volunteers were troubled by the pain they were inflicting, they had been told they were involved in a worthwhile scientific experiment. Studies like this have now been banned in U.S. universities, but they teach us a valuable lesson about why ordinary people sometimes commit horrible human rights abuses.

In times of war, soldiers who are trained to obey orders will behave in ways that they would find unthinkable in other circumstances. At My Lai in 1968, during the Vietnam War, U.S. soldiers obeyed orders given by Lieutenant William Calley to kill hundreds of unarmed men, women, and children at close range.

Soldiers themselves have their rights protected by the Geneva Convention. First written in 1864, it sets out the terms and conditions under which the war wounded and prisoners of war should be properly treated.

▼ *These prisoners were detained during fighting in Afghanistan and are being held at Camp X-Ray at the U.S. naval base in Guantanamo, Cuba. The conditions under which they are being kept may violate the Geneva Convention.*

6. Less Than Human?

Dehumanization

One of the worst cases of human rights abuses the world has ever seen was the Holocaust, the organized genocide of six million Jews, and five million other people including Roma (gypsies), the mentally ill, homosexuals, and communists, by the Nazis during World War II.

The Nazi philosophy was based in part on the ideas of Ernst Rudin. He was a psychiatrist who believed that "inferior" people should be separated from the rest of the population to create a "better" society. This would involve either keeping them in special places and preventing them from having children, or killing them. These chilling ideas were not that unusual in the early part of the 20th century and were fully embraced by the Nazis. In the 1920s and 1930s Germany was in the grip of an economic crisis. The Nazis used people's fears about the economy and the state of the country to turn them against Jews and other minority groups.

▶ *During World War II people were shipped to concentration camps under horrible conditions.*

A grieving woman tends to the grave of her husband, killed in the conflict in Bosnia in the 1990s.

A modern-day holocaust occurred during the war in Bosnia in the 1990s. The Serbian military commander, Ratko Mladic, ordered his troops to bomb particular villages because Muslims lived there. Similarly, in Rwanda in 1994 the government, which was led by people from the Hutu population, ordered the massacre of 800,000 Tutsis. Today, policies and actions such as these that target particular ethnic groups are known as "ethnic cleansing."

This habit of thinking of people who are different as less than human has been a constant problem in human history. This "dehumanization" is a key element in much wartime propaganda. It is the basis of racism and nationalism and makes it much easier to motivate troops to fight. It is also used to justify slavery and racial discrimination.

"They have killed gays and lesbians in Texas because they believe them to be less than human. I believe it is very important that people understand why murders happen and that such murder is a result of hatred ... these murderers were taught to hate by society."

Ann, a human rights campaigner, Texas

In the name of religion?

Article 18 of the UDHR states that "everyone has the right to freedom of thought, conscience, and religion; this right includes freedom to change his religion or belief, and freedom, ... in public or private, to manifest his religion or belief in teaching, practice, worship, and observance."

◀ *An anti-Taliban Afghani fighter prays hours before the end of Ramadan, the Islamic month of fasting, in Afghanistan in 2001.*

Throughout history this right has been denied to many people. For a period of 350 years between the 15th and 19th centuries the Spanish Inquisition ordered the torture and murder of thousands of Spanish Jews, Muslims, Christians, and homosexuals who were punished for not believing in the orthodox Catholic doctrine.

And today, in the 21st century, people still have their right to worship denied to them. In China, members of Falun Gong, a spiritual movement, have been imprisoned for their beliefs by the government. In Tibet, which is governed by China, many Buddhist monasteries have been destroyed and monks have been expelled and taken to China for "re-educating." Some have been tortured for practicing their religion.

In some cases people have tried to force their own religion on others. In 1099 Christian crusaders swept into Jerusalem after a five-week siege and massacred many of the city's Muslims and Jews. They forced their own religion on the rest. More recently, in the 1990s, the Taliban regime in Afghanistan denied young girls the right to go to school and to work. On occasion, it killed men for not attending prayer services.

▼ Under the Taliban rule in Afghanistan all women were required to cover themselves completely by wearing a burqa.

A woman's lot

Women make up half the world's population yet they do two-thirds of the world's work, earn one-tenth of the world's income, and own less than 1 percent of the world's property. And all over the world women contribute hugely to the world's economy through their unpaid work in the home.

Yet in many societies women are considered to be inferior. Around the beginning of the 20th century some psychologists actually believed that women were less highly evolved and less intelligent than men. This theory has been totally disproved, but women still have less power and influence than men in many walks of life.

▲ *This poster in Cambodia warns of the problem of violence against women.*

case study • case study • case study • case study • case study

In April 1999, 29-year-old Samia Sarwar, the mother of two young children, was shot dead in the office of her lawyer in Lahore, Pakistan. She was seeking a divorce after suffering years of violence at the hands of her husband. But, shockingly, her own family was to blame. Family members felt that by seeking a divorce she was bringing dishonor on the family, so they arranged for an assassin to kill her. She was shot in the presence of her own mother and uncle.

The abuse of women's rights is a worldwide problem. Many women are victims of physical abuse committed by their partners at some time in their lives. In many countries the law fails to protect women from this kind of abuse. In the worst cases, women have been killed.

Of course, men are also abused by women. It is often hard for a man claiming to have been abused by his wife to get the police to take his complaint seriously. Similarly, it is often hard for gays and lesbians who have been abused by their partners to get the police to listen to their complaints.

▲ *This Palestinian woman is at a training center. Training programs help women to take control of their lives.*

FACT:
It is estimated that one in four women will experience some form of domestic violence at some point in their lives.

7.Upholding Human Rights

Human rights and international law

Human rights apply to every single person in the world. But human rights are abused all over the world. In some cases the laws of a country are at odds with recognized human rights. For example, some countries have the death penalty, even though that goes against the right to live. Another example may be laws that attempt to stop people from making racist statements—these laws can be seen as going against the right to free speech. This is why international conventions and agreements are so important and so complicated.

Most countries have their own laws that protect people's human rights and they have also signed the various international conventions. But the United States has consistently resisted signing and ratifying the Convention on the Rights of the Child, claiming that their own domestic laws are adequate. It resents what it sees as interference from the international community.

◀ *Women at a literacy class in Bengal, India. Women in many countries learn to read and write as adults because the right to education was denied them when they were young.*

▲ *Slobodan Milosevic on trial for crimes against humanity at the International Criminal Tribunal for the Former Yugoslavia.*

The United States has been reluctant to support the establishment of an International Criminal Court. This court would punish leaders of countries that abuse human rights and would prosecute people accused of genocide, crimes against humanity, and war crimes. The United States thinks the court may be used to accuse U.S. soldiers of abuses.

On an individual level it is important that people learn what their rights are and become able to challenge those who try to take them away.

> "We must rid this planet of the obscenity that a person stands a better chance of being tried and judged for killing one human being than for killing 100,000."
>
> *Jose Ayala-Lasso, UN Commissioner for Human Rights, 1996*

Conflicting human rights

Some people believe that everyone should be free to do as they choose, as long as they do not interfere with the freedom of others. But human rights often conflict with each other and with people's beliefs and faiths and national laws. Sometimes these conflicts prevent human rights from being upheld.

The right to freedom of expression or a fair trial may clash with the right to privacy. Celebrities often see the freedom of the press as infringing on their right to privacy. The right to cultural or religious practice may clash with the right not to be discriminated against. The rights to a healthy environment, education, health care, or welfare benefits may be in competition with one another over the same limited resources.

◀ Some people claim that Princess Diana's death was caused because her car was being chased by press photographers. She often complained that her right to privacy was invaded by photographers.

▲ In China families are only permitted to have one child. The government argues that this is in the best interests of the majority.

Conflicts often arise between individual and group human rights. In order to feed its rapidly growing population, in 1980 China introduced a "One Child Policy." Every birth had to be approved by family planning officials. The family received free education, housing, pension, and other benefits but these were withdrawn if they had a second child.

In a similar way some countries, such as Australia and Belgium, demand compulsory voting in general elections. The purpose is to ensure democracy, but is it an infringement of someone's freedom to force them to vote?

Bystander or activist?

It is easy to think that none of us will abuse someone else's human rights. But there is a famous saying: "All that is needed for evil to prevail is for good people to do nothing." In other words, failing to take action against someone who is abusing rights can be as bad as deliberately abusing human rights yourself. We all have to take responsibility for the consequences of our actions and ensure that we are not harming others. We can also seek out ways in which we can guarantee the human rights of others.

In 1995 the United Nations sent peacekeeping forces into Bosnia to protect the local population that was being threatened by Serbian forces. The Dutch forces were accused of human rights abuses for not doing enough to protect the population of the town of Srebrenica. Up to 8,000 Muslim men and boys were executed by Serb soldiers while the Dutch UN contingent did nothing to save them.

▶ Dutch UN peacekeeping forces rest next to Bosnian refugees from Srebrenica, 1995. The Dutch troops did not prevent the killing of Muslims who were under their care.

Businesses can be guilty of indirectly abusing the human rights of their country's own military forces. In the late 1980s, U.S. and European countries sold chemical and biological weapons to Iraq. Since the Gulf War, more than one in three of the U.S. troops who served there have sought medical care for undiagnosed problems, believed by some people to be related to exposures to these toxic chemicals.

Human rights cannot be guarded simply by individuals, businesses, and the state not interfering with individual freedoms. The human rights of people have to be actively fought and campaigned for.

▲ *Driving while drunk endangers other people's human rights. This is a memorial to a victim of a drunk driver in California. The organization Mothers Against Drunk Drivers (MADD) was set up to draw attention to this problem.*

"Rights for too many remain little more than words on paper. However, I do believe that we should commit ourselves to focusing on the future, reinvigorating the common will and commitment of the international community to ensuring the enjoyment of human rights by people everywhere. We are all custodians of human rights and we must find our own way to do what is required."

Mary Robinson, High Commissioner for Human Rights, United Nations

GLOSSARY

adultery
sexual relationships outside marriage

apartheid
segregation of a population on the basis of race

atrocity
cruel and inhumane deed

capital punishment
act of putting someone convicted of a crime to death

capitalism
economic system that depends on the private ownership of property

censorship
banning of certain information from being published or broadcast

civil rights
rights that all citizens have. They include legal, economic, and social rights

civil rights movement
campaign to secure equal rights for African Americans in the United States

civilian
someone who is not connected with the military forces of a country

conventions
international agreements

curfew
order stating the time by which people must be at home

democracy
government elected by the people; from the Greek word *demos,* which means "people" and *kratos,* which means "rule."

discrimination
unfair treatment of someone usually because of their race, gender, sexual orientation, or disability

doctrine
set of beliefs

ethnic cleansing
act of mass expulsion or killing of people from ethnic or religious groups in a certain area

euthanasia
act of killing someone painlessly, often because they are suffering an incurable illness. Sometimes called "mercy killing."

genocide
mass killing of a particular racial or cultural group

Holocaust
extermination of eleven million Jews, Roma (gypsies), mentally ill, and homosexual people by the Nazis during World War II. When holocaust is spelled with a small "h" it means any mass destruction.

labor union
organization set up to protect the rights of workers

massacre
mass murder

minority group
group of people who are different from the larger group of which they are a part

nationalism
feeling that people in a country or area all belong together and are different from people in other places. Also used to describe a belief in the superiority of your own country or ethnicity.

negotiate
to discuss something with another party in order to reach an agreement

pacifist
someone who is opposed to all forms of violence

paramilitary
group of people who are not in the armed forces, but who are organized and behave like a military unit

parole
to release a prisoner before his or her sentence is complete on the promise of good behavior. People on parole are still checked on by the authorities.

ratification
formal approval and granting of legal authority to a document

refugee
someone who is forced to leave his or her home and country against his or her will

segregated
being forced to lead a life separate from other people

sterilization
operation that prevents women from getting pregnant

universal
something that applies to everyone in the world

FURTHER INFORMATION

BOOKS TO READ

Altman, Linda Jacobs. *Human Rights: Issues for a New Millenium.* Berkeley Heights, N.J.: Enslow, 2002.

Hossell, Karen Price. *The Bill of Rights.* Chicago: Heinemann, 2003.

Immell, Myra. *Ethnic Violence.* Farmington Hills, Mich.: Gale Group, 2000.

January, Brendan. *Civil Rights.* Chicago: Heinemann, 2004.

Stearman, Kaye. *Women's Rights.* Chicago: Raintree, 2000.

The entire text of the Universal Declaration of Human Rights (in several languages, including English) can be found on the Internet at: www.unhcr.ch/udhr/.

A version written in simple to understand language is available at: www.un.org/cyberschoolbus/humanrights/resources/plainchild.asp.

ORGANIZATIONS

American Anti-Slavery Group
189 Tremont Street #421
Boston, MA 02116
www.iabolish.com

American Red Cross
431 18th Street NW
Washington, DC 20006
www.redcross.org

Amnesty International USA
322 Eighth Avenue
New York, NY 10001
www.amnestyusa.org

Oxfam America
26 West Street
Boston, MA 02111
www.oxfamamerica.org

Save the Children
2000 M Street NW, Suite 500
Washington, DC 20036
www.savethechildren.org

UNHCR (The UN Refugee Agency)
United Nations High Commissioner
for Refugees
Case Postale 2500
CH-1211 Geneve 2 Depot
Switzerland
www.unhcr.ch

INDEX